Pianoworks
Popular Styles

Janet and Alan Bullard

MUSIC DEPARTMENT

OXFORD
UNIVERSITY PRESS

OXFORD
UNIVERSITY PRESS

Great Clarendon Street, Oxford OX2 6DP, England

Oxford University Press is a department of the University of Oxford.
It furthers the University's aim of excellence in research, scholarship,
and education by publishing worldwide

Oxford is a registered trade mark of Oxford University Press
in the UK and in certain other countries

3 5 7 9 10 8 6 4 2

ISBN: 978-0-19-339816-0

Music and text origination by Julia Bovee
Printed in Great Britain on acid-free paper by
Halstan & Co. Ltd., Amersham, Bucks.

Contents

Up River

Janet and Alan Bullard

Moderate; gently swaying (quavers may be swung ♫ = ♪♪)

una corda

Written in close-harmony style, this piece evokes a rowing boat slowly navigating a twisting and turning river. Follow the dynamics carefully to help convey a sense of flow. Whether you play with straight or swing quavers, keep the rhythm positive and avoid hurrying.

Back Street Band

Janet and Alan Bullard

Powerfully, with a rock feel

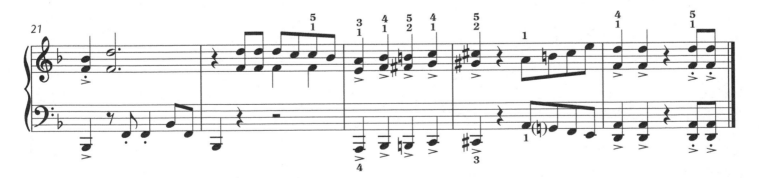

This piece, like many rock numbers, is based on a simple rhythmic groove in the left hand. You could start by practising this groove on its own, so that the rhythm is confident before you add the right-hand melody.

Satin

Janet and Alan Bullard

Rhythmic but expressive (quavers may be swung ♩ = ♪♪)

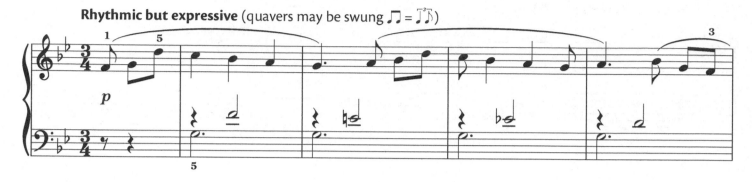

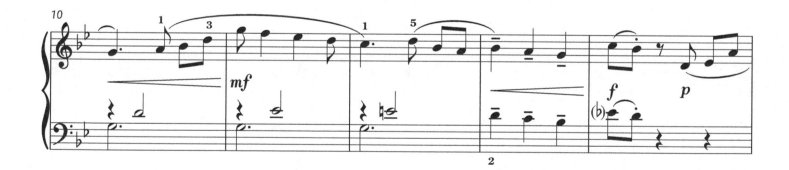

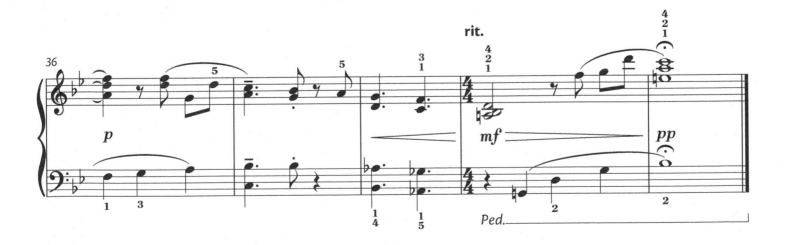

Aim for a smooth, flowing feel in this gentle jazz waltz. Maintain the pulse steadily and clearly in your head, aiming for rhythmic continuity in bars 6, 17, and similar places.

Dovedale

Janet and Alan Bullard

Expressive and smooth

con Ped. (opt.)

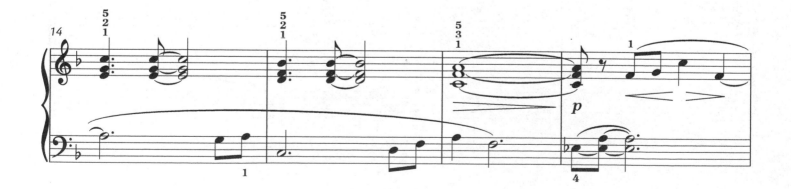

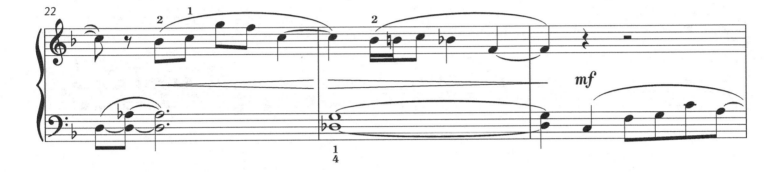

Dovedale is a wooded valley, overlooked by high cliffs, in Derbyshire's Peak District. An expressive tone will help to convey the changing beauty of this landscape. The middle section (bars 17–24) can be delicate in feeling, with gentle semiquaver ornaments. Careful use of the sustaining pedal will enhance the texture, for example in the opening bars.

Model T

Janet and Alan Bullard

Jauntily

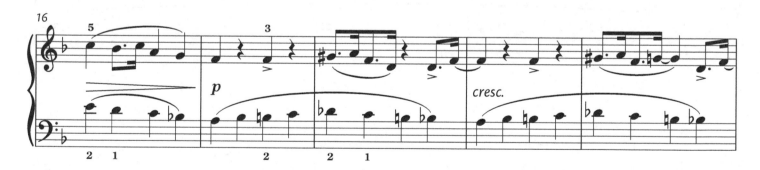

With a hint of old-time blues, this rhythmic piece evokes 1920s America and the ubiquitous Ford Model T car. Set a steady tempo—rhythmic but unhurried—as if to suggest a weekend drive.

Airborne

Janet and Alan Bullard

Most of this gentle piece is in the Dorian mode (the scale of D without any sharps or flats), which helps to create a feeling of floating in the air. The marked pedalling, except for the last two bars, is optional. In all the pedalled bars, you could try holding down all the left-hand notes until the end of the bar, to enrich the texture. In bars 9–16 the unexpected chords suggest a change of mood—take care not to hurry here.

Thames Sunrise

Janet and Alan Bullard

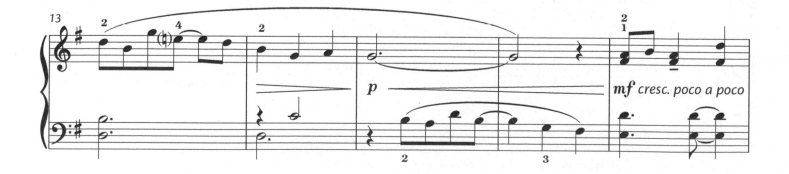

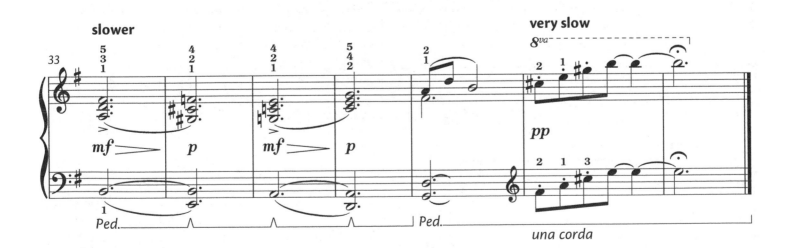

Play this evocative ballad with colour and character, and make the melody sing. The staccato quavers at the end should be played very lightly, using both pedals, to create a misty sonority.

Kaleidoscope

Janet and Alan Bullard

Andantino espressivo, con poco rubato

Kaleidoscope

Janet and Alan Bullard

Andantino espressivo, con poco rubato

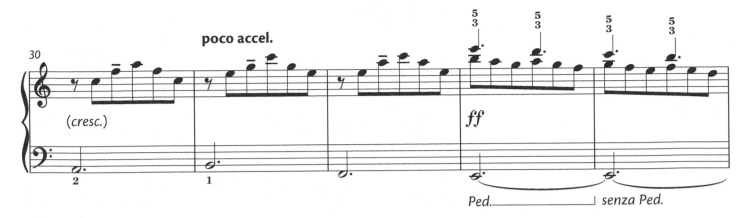

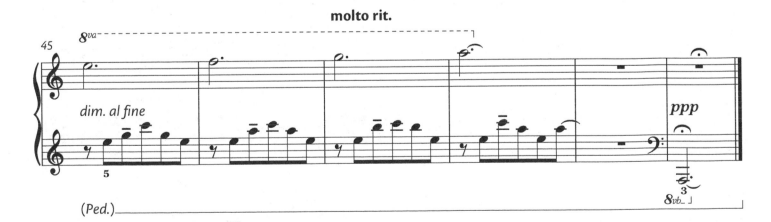

Suggested by the changing reflections as you gently turn a kaleidoscope, this piece explores the sonorities of the piano. The second quaver in most bars is indicated by a tenuto and should be played with a little more weight. In bars 10–12 and 22–4, cross the left hand over the right hand and aim for a gentle, bell-like staccato touch with the 2nd finger. Notice the commas every so often—imagine you are taking a breath (releasing the pedal) before the next phrase. Hold down the sustaining and *una corda* pedals from bar 40 until the end.

My Shout!

Janet and Alan Bullard

'Shout' is a lively style of gospel music featuring short phrases, like a conversation. Notice the details in the articulation, and aim to keep the rhythm really tight to help communicate a sense of excitement.

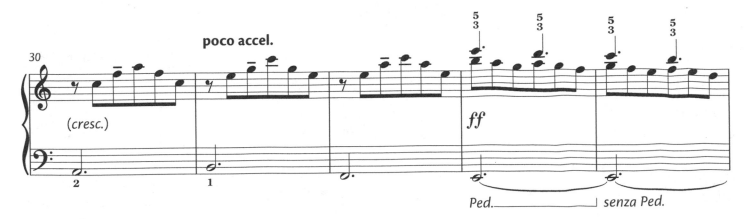

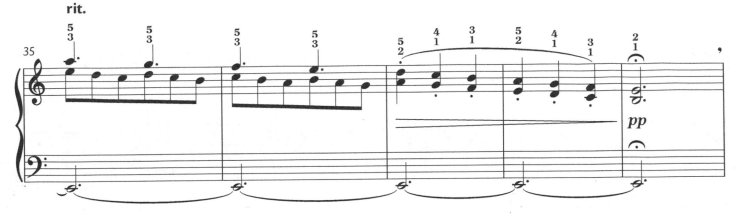

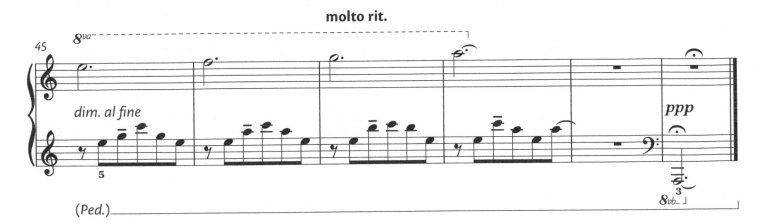

Suggested by the changing reflections as you gently turn a kaleidoscope, this piece explores the sonorities of the piano. The second quaver in most bars is indicated by a tenuto and should be played with a little more weight. In bars 10–12 and 22–4, cross the left hand over the right hand and aim for a gentle, bell-like staccato touch with the 2nd finger. Notice the commas every so often—imagine you are taking a breath (releasing the pedal) before the next phrase. Hold down the sustaining and *una corda* pedals from bar 40 until the end.

My Shout!

Janet and Alan Bullard

Punchy

'Shout' is a lively style of gospel music featuring short phrases, like a conversation. Notice the details in the articulation, and aim to keep the rhythm really tight to help communicate a sense of excitement.

poco accel.

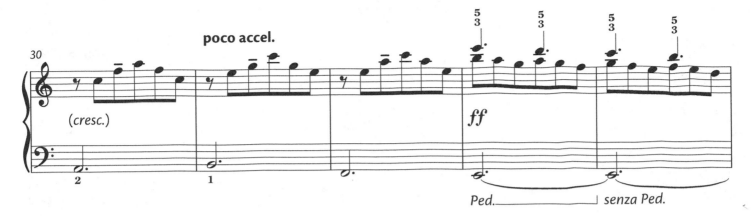

(cresc.)

ff

Ped._____⌐ senza Ped.

rit.

pp

a tempo, calmly

una corda
Ped.____

molto rit.

dim. al fine

ppp

(Ped.)____

Suggested by the changing reflections as you gently turn a kaleidoscope, this piece explores the sonorities of the piano. The second quaver in most bars is indicated by a tenuto and should be played with a little more weight. In bars 10–12 and 22–4, cross the left hand over the right hand and aim for a gentle, bell-like staccato touch with the 2nd finger. Notice the commas every so often—imagine you are taking a breath (releasing the pedal) before the next phrase. Hold down the sustaining and *una corda* pedals from bar 40 until the end.

My Shout!

Janet and Alan Bullard

Punchy

'Shout' is a lively style of gospel music featuring short phrases, like a conversation. Notice the details in the articulation, and aim to keep the rhythm really tight to help communicate a sense of excitement.

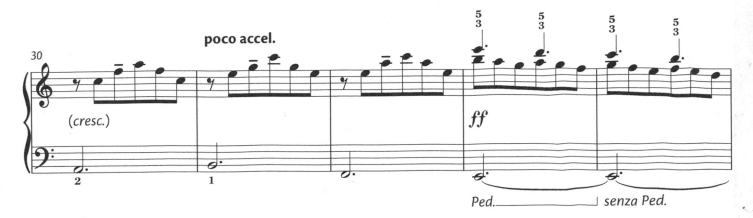

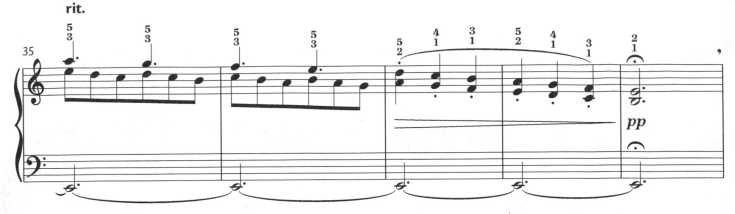

Suggested by the changing reflections as you gently turn a kaleidoscope, this piece explores the sonorities of the piano. The second quaver in most bars is indicated by a tenuto and should be played with a little more weight. In bars 10–12 and 22–4, cross the left hand over the right hand and aim for a gentle, bell-like staccato touch with the 2nd finger. Notice the commas every so often—imagine you are taking a breath (releasing the pedal) before the next phrase. Hold down the sustaining and *una corda* pedals from bar 40 until the end.

My Shout!

Janet and Alan Bullard

Punchy

'Shout' is a lively style of gospel music featuring short phrases, like a conversation. Notice the details in the articulation, and aim to keep the rhythm really tight to help communicate a sense of excitement.

Azalea

Adagio espressivo

Janet and Alan Bullard

con Ped.

poco rit.

poco più mosso

poco rit.

molto rit.

a tempo

relaxed

Ped._____

rit. al fine

Suggesting, perhaps, a colourful floral display, this piece should be played with an expressively singing melody, whichever hand it is in. Keep the accompanying crotchets quieter than the melody, but always 'lean' on the tenutos, making the most of the big dynamic climax in bar 13 and the contrasting calm of the final bars. Be sure to use the sustaining pedal as marked in bars 13–15, to allow the sonorities to build up.

Café Colombia

Janet and Alan Bullard

With energy

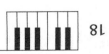

Aim for precision, with absolutely even quavers, in this lively Latin American-style dance. In the sections where the musical line is shared between the staves, keep the wrists up and forward to avoid collisions. Look out for the changing key signatures, and make the rhythm tight and sparkling.

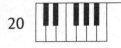

Sycamore

Janet and Alan Bullard

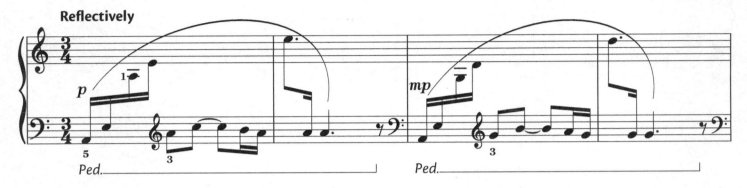

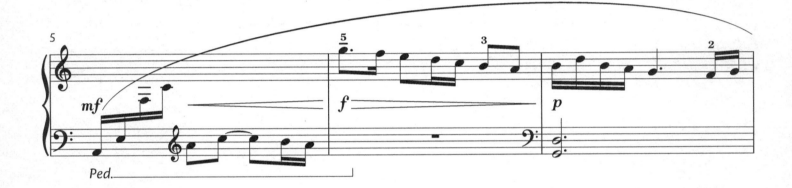

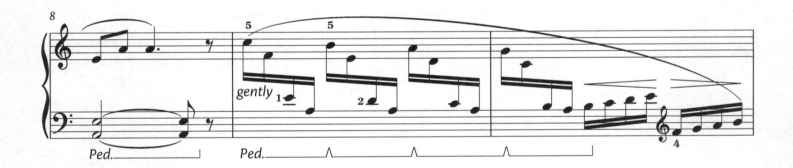

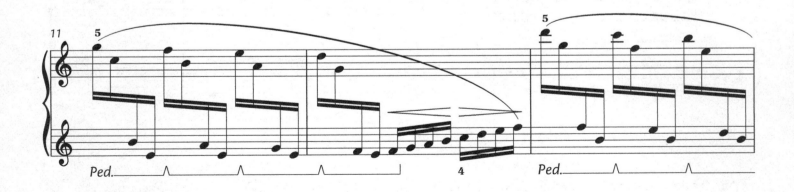

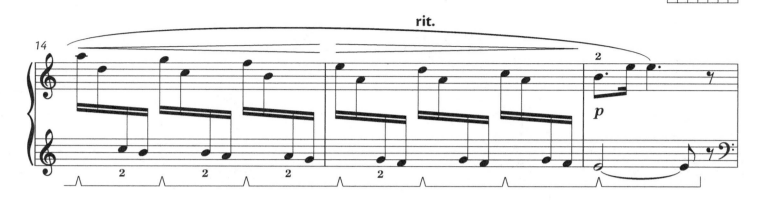

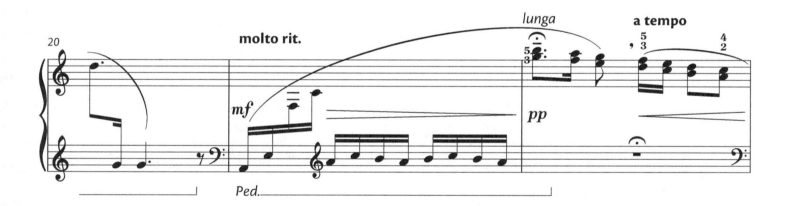

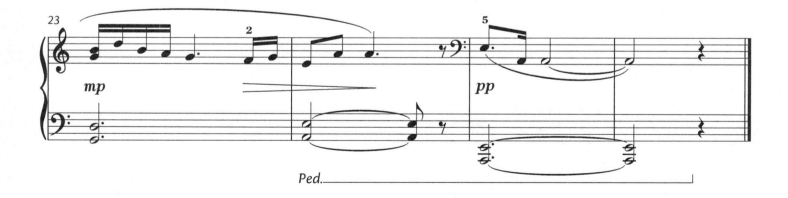

In this evocative piece, the crossing hands mirror the sycamore seed as it rises and falls in the breeze. Aim for graceful movements, delicate pedalling, and precise balance between the hands—and make the pause in bar 22 last as long as you like!

Brighton Belle

Janet and Alan Bullard

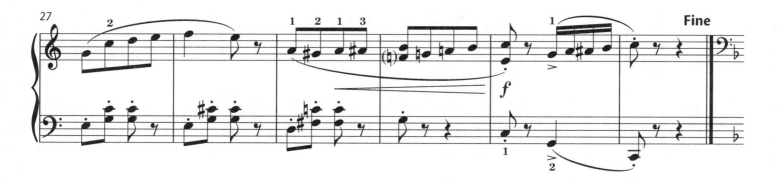

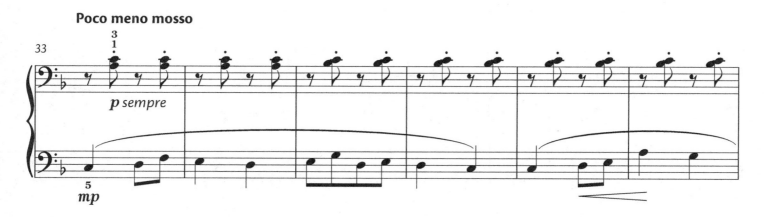

The 'Brighton Belle' was a luxury electric express train that ran between London and Brighton during the last century. It featured in the 1953 film *London to Brighton in Four Minutes*—shot from the driver's cab throughout the hour-long journey and speeded up with trick photography. Keep the staccato quavers very light, and in the second section (bars 33–48) make sure the right hand is played **p** throughout, allowing the left hand to come through expressively—think cellos!

Night Waves

Janet and Alan Bullard

Flowing blues feel

una corda

In this haunting piece, tinged with elements of the blues, aim for a delicate legato where indicated, and clearly differentiate the tenutos and staccatos. It's not essential to use the sustaining pedal, but you could add a touch on the tenuto crotchets. Play the grace notes gently to add colour to the repeated phrases, and add more elsewhere if you like! Keep a steady pulse throughout, without hurrying.

Moonlight Through Glass

Janet and Alan Bullard

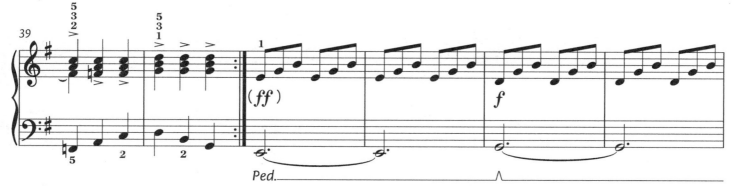

This piece responds to the opening bars of Beethoven's 'Moonlight' Sonata through the repetitive style of American minimalist composers. Whatever speed you choose, ensure that the quavers are steady and regular. Note the sudden cut-off at the end of the piece—take care not to slow down here. Make the dynamic contrasts as marked as you can, using the sustaining pedal as directed to enrich the sound.

Radical Riffs

Janet and Alan Bullard

Lively, with humour

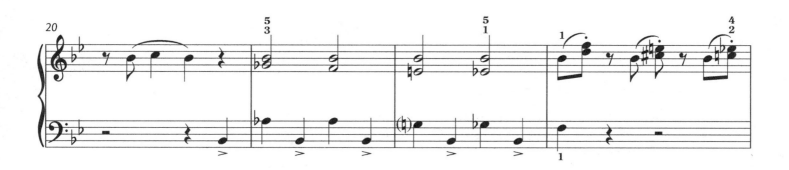

There's a touch of the New Orleans traditional jazz style here, with the use of short rhythmic shapes ('riffs') and a number of 'blue' notes. Remember to count right through the rests so that the rhythmic shape is always clear, to help emphasize the musical humour.

Just One Day

Janet and Alan Bullard

Gently and wistfully, poco rubato

una corda

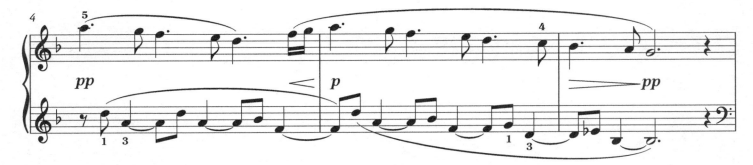

con Ped.

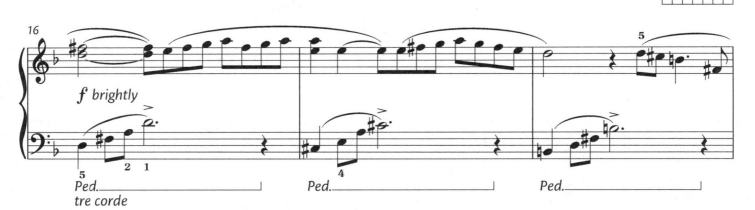

This miniature could be a film score, with many stories to tell. To help communicate the dramatic changes in musical mood and colour, follow the pedal markings—lowering the *una corda* pedal at the beginning and raising it at *tre corde*—and aim for a full tone in the *f* and *ff* passages.

Postlude

Janet and Alan Bullard

This lively study in the neo-classical style, using Baroque-inspired fragments within a more modern context, requires agile and precise finger-work. Use the pedal only in the last two bars.